HAUNTED
HAMPTONS

HAUNTED HAMPTONS

LONG ISLAND'S
SOUTH FORK PHANTOMS

LYNDA LEE MACKEN

Haunted Hamptons: Long Island's South Fork Phantoms

Published by
Black Cat Press
Post Office Box 1466
Point Pleasant Beach, NJ 08742

ISBN 978-1-7360069-4-8

Book & Cover Design by Deb Tremper, Six Penny Graphics.
www.sixpennygraphics.com.

CONTENTS

INTRODUCTION

The Hamptons consist of towns, villages, and hamlets, on the eastern end of Long Island. Most famously, the scenic region is *the* place to enjoy cool ocean breezes, white sand beaches, succulent seafood, lively parties, and *ghosts*! The Hamptons exist as one of the most *haunted* summer colonies of the northeastern United States!

Haunted Hamptons explores the South Forks' supernatural side, blending ancient spirits with modern day specters to chronicle the haven's intriguing tales and legends. Lighthouses, mansions, restaurants and resorts, historic homes, and even a haunted windmill, tingle with otherworldly energies that startle the unsuspecting and mystify the living.

Everything in nature possesses a life force including water. The Hamptons' location by the sea offers spirits opportunities to appear by using the water's energy. Spirits utilize water as an energy source to help with communication. Even rain or storms can empower spirits to manifest. Also, when close to a body of water, senses are heightened, enabling greater contact with other dimensions. Water is a powerful conductor between worlds.

The Hampton's haunted history dates to its Native American

inhabitants. Chilling tribal legends flourish while restless natives seek peace at Montauk Manor. English settlers lived and died here—some left their essence behind and still frequent their ancient dwellings, such as scalping victim Elizabeth at the Halsey House. Extraordinary tales of early colonists such as Elizabeth Halsey Wheeler can cause a shiver or two.

Some paranormal researchers contend that ghosts are the spirits of the dead who for some reason are "stuck" between this plane of existence and the next, often as a result of some tragedy or trauma. Ghost hunters and psychic mediums say such earth-bound spirits are confused and don't realize they're dead.

Some who met with a sudden end can remain in a state of shock keeping them trapped in the mortal world. The ghost appears to exist in an in-between state, living in two worlds simultaneously, and haunts the place where they died, or other meaningful locations. This type of ghost usually interacts with the living and reacts to being seen.

On crossing over, there are those, who because of strong emotional ties to the earth plane, fail to move on to the other realm. Some psychic mediums or sensitive individuals who communicate across dimensions will help the puzzled spirits by explaining that their physical bodies are dead and encouraging them to enter the spirit phase of their existence.

"Ghosts are memories."
—Scott Milligan, Physical Medium

Viewers of the popular TV show *Ghost Hunters* are familiar with the term "residual hauntings." This type of haunting is like a recording on the environment where the individual once existed. Strong emotions imprint indelible impressions on a location which can produce a residual haunting. This occurs where an event is so embedded, it replays over and over, trapped in time, similar to an endless audio or video tape. The individual's life force is not actually present, only the energy of the event remains impressed on the ethers. These ghostly sensations can repeat for decades or longer.

Mrs. Cordelia, or Mary, Rogers' ghost roaming the confines of her Southampton home, is an example of a residual haunting, for example. As is Beatrice Clafin's ghostly giggle that echoes in the Mill Hill windmill where she often played. The entities' appearance and actions are the same over and over again—leftover energies replaying.

Lighthouses exist as beacons of hope to lost sailors, but some own a shadow side. Every lighthouse seems to hold a ghostly inhabitant... or two! Such is the case at the Montauk Point Lighthouse where ghostly energies radiate.

Glimpses of the past—traumatic recreations, emotional events or even footsteps up and down a hallway are common to many of the Hamptons' haunted places. The impressive apparitions at Sanderling, Southampton's Rogers House, Billy Joel's or Renée Zellweger's former homes, or Grey Gardens exist as consequential memories.

How the energies are recorded and *why* they replay continuously remains a mystery. Whatever the mechanics, the astounding hauntings continue...

EASTPORT

LLOYD'S ANTIQUES

496 Montauk Parkway

For decades, Lloyd's Antiques existed in a three-story, 10,000-square-foot concrete building in downtown Eastport. The long-time antique store held more than ancient artifacts and curios. On the word of proprietor Lloyd Gerard, the place housed the spirit of Gerard's four times great uncle Andrew Simon Levi.

In 1998, Gerard shared some interesting family history with *Newsday* staff writer Jerry Zezima along with a bit of mystery that surrounded the strange events transpiring in the shop.

Andrew Simon Levi immigrated from Russia in 1860 and made a living on Long Island peddling goods to farmers and their families. Levi wore a rucksack and lugged two suitcases full of household necessities such as pots, pans, needles, and pins "from Brooklyn to Montauk to Greenport to Orient." Levi's sales route took two months to complete and when he finished his circuit he trudged back to New York City, replenished his inventory, and began his route all over again.

Gerard's grandfather, Harry Goldstein, once owned the building that housed Lloyd's Antiques and he pedaled goods with Uncle Levi until he married and settled in Eastport. It appeared that Uncle Levi, however, continued his sales pitch from the other side.

Once a customer came back to the store to purchase a $65 table he saw on the second floor the week before. Gerrard was puzzled—the table was priced at $400. When the buyer related the encounter with a bearded old man, Gerard realized the patron described Uncle Levi! Gerard sold the table for $65, pleasing Uncle Levi no doubt.

150 years ago, Uncle Levi walked for miles to make a sale, but for decades Uncle Levi's sales territory was the antique shop's second floor! Several people witnessed the man's apparition peering out over the town from the second story, picture window.

According to Gerard, his easygoing uncle liked to play practical jokes. When books flew off their shelves or other merchandise moved around, Gerard blamed his long-ago relation and felt that Uncle Levi merely continued his business from beyond the grave.

QUOGUE

SANDERLING

BEACH LANE

Private Residence

In 1745, Maurice Avison commissioned the building of Blake Hall in Mirfield, Yorkshire, England. English novelist and poet Anne Brontë served as governess to the Ingham family who lived there in the early 1800s. After only nine months, Anne left the manse with a distaste for child care; she was 19 years old.

Brontë depicts her experiences of living in Blake Hall in two of her novels entitled, *Agnes Grey* and *The Tenant of Wildfell Hall*. Brontë used pseudonyms in the stories inspired by her tenure with the Inghams.

One of the outstanding features of the home was the Queen Anne staircase. Hand carved from rare, burled yew, when Blake Hall was razed, workers dismantled the flight of steps, and the stairs went up for auction. A London antiques dealer placed the highest bid and won the staircase.

Four years later, opera singer Gladys Topping and her husband Allen, were visiting London and attended the

Kensington Antique Fair. The couple sought furnishings for their house in Quogue which was built in 1954. When one of the dealers showed them the elegant stairway from Blake Hall, the Toppings immediately purchased the one-of-a-kind staircase for their Long Island house on Ogden Pond.

In 1965, *The Mirfield Reporter* stated that the widowed Mrs. Topping observed a young woman ascending the stairs. The figure wore a long, full skirt, triangle shawl, and her hair was styled in a bun. Mrs. Topping described the female apparition as looking pensive. When Topping tried to verbally soothe her agitated dog, Mr. Wyk, who also witnessed the spirit, the figure disappeared. Topping intuited the diaphanous apparition was Anne Brontë's ghost. Later she heard disembodied rapping and footsteps, though Anne did not reveal herself again.

Stairways are high traffic areas and therefore hold a lot of energy. These established pathways store the energy of days gone by and somehow replay it for us to see, hear or feel in the form of paranormal phenomena.

Mrs. Topping visited the moors around Brontë's home in Haworth, England to walk in the author's footsteps. Perhaps Mrs. Topping's affinity with Brontë enabled her to sense often Anne's presence in the house.

> *"We meet them at the door-way, on the stair,*
> *Along the passages they come and go,*
> *Impalpable impressions on the air,*
> *A sense of something moving to and fro."*
> —HENRY WADSWORTH LONGFELLOW

HAMPTON BAYS

VILLA PAUL RESTAURANT

162 W Montauk Highway

I n 1804, Joseph and Phebe Brown built a log cabin on the site of today's Villa Paul Restaurant. The couple existed as farmers and gave birth to four children. The current Men's and Women's rooms in Villa Paul consist of the original, Brown family home; this section served as the "borning room." Borning rooms were also known as "birthing rooms" and were common in 19th century era houses. Reserved solely for birth, illness, and death, the special chambers provided both an entrance and an exit to this life.[1]

Judge Edward Lazansky, served as Justice of the New York Supreme Court from 1920–1940, among other high political offices he held throughout his lifetime. His wife Cora may be responsible for the eerie happenings reported at the restaurant.

After her husband's death, Cora wanted to sell the

1 HISTORY | Mysite (villapaulrestaurant.com)

property. She considered that prospective buyers might be put off by the property's location next to Danes Cemetery. Cora solved the potential problem by removing the headstones thereby hiding the graveyard. In doing so, the location of bodies became unknown, loved ones' remains now rested in unmarked graves.

The community flew into an uproar but to no avail.

Paul Villa converted the Lazansky's abandoned mansion into Villa Paul Restaurant. The room that housed Judge Lazansky's library serves as the main dining room. Since 1965, the Pensa family has owned and operated the restaurant.

Mrs. Lazansky's inconceivable gravestone robbery may be the cause of the haunting, which includes disembodied footsteps and lights going on and off on their own. Diners and staffers witnessed a spectral female thought to be the judge's wife. Even a phantom dog occasionally runs through the dining room at this popular eatery.

CANOE
PLACE INN

According to the Hampton Bays Historical Society, the Canoe Place Inn is the most storied property in Hampton Bays.

In the 1600s, the structure existed as a dwelling in the wilderness between Riverhead and Southampton and the house also served as a trading post.

In 1739, Jeremiah Culver, one of the area's earliest settlers, bought the property. He operated a stagecoach stop and tavern making the Canoe Place Inn the oldest hostelry in America. The property was called the "canoe place" because it was a popular location for Native Americans to launch their canoes and access Shinnecock Bay.

During the Revolutionary War, the property functioned as a British fort. Several hundred troops were stationed on the hill behind the inn.

With the coming of the railroad in the 1880s, came the tourists. Boarding houses and hotels proliferated at the time for visitors traveling from the city.

In 1902, the Buchmuller family, owners of the Waldorf Astoria in Manhattan, operated the inn. Ernest Buchmuller charged guests a rate based on the model of car they drove.

Stocked with liquor by bootleggers, Canoe Place Inn drew crowds during Prohibition. The inn became a popular destination for notables such as actresses Helen Hayes and Lucille Ball, and former President Franklin D. Roosevelt. Canoe Place became a stop along the Montauk Branch of the Long Island Railroad and ran "Fisherman's Special" trains.

According to locals, ghostly apparitions often appeared in the inn's weathered windows.

The original Canoe Place Inn burned to the ground on July 5, 1921. Two staff members, Florence Whittington, a maid, and cashier Richard Heineman, died in the blaze. Three guests, along with a maid, jumped out of windows to escape their deaths. Ms. Whittington stared beseechingly out a third-floor window, but onlookers were powerless to save her.

The room where Ms. Whittington perished became the epicenter of the haunting activity as some believe her spirit continued on at the inn. A strange light emanated from the third story window where Ms. Whittington succumbed.

The inn reopened its doors in 1922 and hosted a variety of entertainers including Duke Ellington, Jefferson Starship, Jon Bon Jovi, and Billy Joel, among others.

A new era began at the Canoe Place Inn after a major rehabilitation returned the inn to its early-to-mid 20th-century appearance complete with modern amenities. Will Ms. Whittington move on or linger at her old digs? Only time will tell.

Moonlight on the Shore, Long Island.

WRECK OF THE
LOUIS V. PLACE

*On February 8, 1895, all but two crew members froze
to death in the rigging of the* Louis V. Place.

Patchogue's Lakeview Cemetery is the final resting place
for the sailors who froze to death on the schooner *Louis
V. Place* during a fierce winter storm on February 8, 1895. The
Brooklyn Daily Eagle newspaper chronicled the tragedy and
the startling aftermath.

As the 163-foot, ice-encrusted schooner foundered off the coast, Captain William H. Squires ordered his crew to put on as much clothing as they could manage and advised swigging whiskey for warmth. He instructed the men to secure themselves in the three-masted ship's rigging to stay high above the icy waters smashing the struggling vessel.

Six of the eight seafarers froze to death by the time a rescue boat reached them. Four of the dead, including the Captain, fell into the sea. Two men dangled in the ship's ropes, frozen to death. Two were rescued but one died. The lone survivor explained that he crawled into the furled topsail to escape the brutal winds.

The 19th century newspaper article reported that every evening a ghostly form rose from the men's graves. A low, eerie moan preceded the appearance of the strange mist. Then the specter floated over to a tree and flailed about as if signaling for help. Was the ghost recreating his last moments?

Thirteen days after the grounding off Sayville, Captain Squires' corpse drifted home to Good Ground, today's Hampton Bays. The sea captain's frozen cadaver drifted 30 miles *against* the current before it reached his birthplace. His body landed only yards from his home.

Captain Squires once served as an assistant lighthouse keeper at Shinnecock Light. The man who once worked at a guiding light was himself guided back to his family. By all accounts his mystical, final journey defies explanation.

SOUTHAMPTON

MILL HILL
WINDMILL

239 Montauk Highway

Eastern Long Island boasts the largest collection of
surviving windmills in the United States. Looked upon
as picturesque and quaint relics of the past, windmills are
engineering marvels and functioned as vital labor-saving
devices for early settlers. They facilitated grinding corn
and grain, pumping water, sawing wood, and various other
essential chores.

The Stony Brook Southampton campus windmill, situated
on a knoll overlooking Shinnecock Hills, is known historically
as the Mill Hill windmill and originally stood behind Windmill
Lane in Southampton village. Constructed in 1712, and restored
by Stony Brook University in 2006, the building features ornate
woodwork and two operational hearths.

The three story, grey shingle structure served as a landmark
for seafarers until Mrs. William S. Hoyt, the daughter of
Abraham Lincoln's secretary of the Navy Salmon P. Chase,

purchased the windmill in 1890 and moved the artifact to her property for use as a tearoom and playhouse. A team of horses pulled the historic structure to its present location.

Six years later, wealthy textile manufacturer Arthur B. Claflin, purchased the Hoyt property and constructed a 30-room summer "cottage." The interior workings of the picturesque windmill were removed, and the gutted mill became transformed into a unique lodge for guests and afternoon tea. In 1957, playwright Tennessee Williams wrote *The Day on Which a Man Dies* while staying at the windmill. The story concerned his friend, painter Jackson Pollock, who was killed in a car crash the year before.

There seems to be a spectral occupant who lingers inside the weathered space—the spirit of a little girl.

Claflin's daughter Beatrice loved to frolic in the distinctive structure. The word is that her play turned tragic when she fell down the steep stairs, broke her neck and died from her injuries.

As maintained by untold students the young girl's ghost inhabits her playhouse, her innocent face often peers from the pint-sized windows. Captivated students say they feel her presence and assert that the windmill generates a supernatural vibe.

Electromagnetic field detection meters are used to seek out disruptions in the natural magnetic field of the environment. They help to authenticate evidence of paranormal activity. Ghost hunters' meters register an unusually high magnetic field on the windmill's hill.

Undergrads sense someone staring at them as they pass

the place at night and insist a tiny indistinct voice calls out to them. Sensitive students get the impression that the spirit of Claflin's lonely daughter is looking for a playmate.

The girl's apparition appears in every window and because of her diminutive size, only her head and shoulders are visible. The tiny face follows passersby, gazing out at them from window to window.

The historic, picturesque windmill endures as the symbol of Southampton Stony Brook signifying the history and traditions of eastern Long Island, its petite phantom presence, a sad and lonely reminder of its tragic past.

ROGERS MANSION

17 Meeting House Lane

The Rogers Mansion is a Greek Revival style home that today serves as the headquarters for the Southampton Historical Museum. Whaling Captain Albert Rogers built the white clapboard edifice in 1843, and lived there with his family until his death in 1854. The house went up on land deeded to the Rogers family in 1644 and descendants occupied the house until 1889.

In 1899, well-known philanthropist Samuel Longstreth Parrish purchased the property from Rogers' descendants and expanded the structure in 1911.

Eventually the mansion housed the offices of the Red Cross, YMCA, and finally a historical museum. For many years, staffers noticed unexplainable phenomena at their workplace.

The disturbing sound of furniture being moved overhead, when the second floor stood vacant, raised goosebumps. Disembodied footsteps echoing down hallways made the staff shiver. Wafts of ice-cold air gave the workers chills. Who made noises in the empty attic? What caused the noise of a cacophony of people when no one was there? Is it the shadow forms some see in their peripheral vision?

The museum contacted Long Island Paranormal Investigators who used state of the art equipment to capture evidence of the paranormal. When the ghost hunters reviewed all the data they collected, they declared the mansion *haunted*.

The sighting of a female apparition haunting the old mansion sealed the deal. The bona-fide ghost is thought to be either Cordelia Rogers, Captains Rogers' second wife, or Mary Rogers, his first wife, Cordelia's sister. [2]

When Cordelia Rogers passed away she was waked in the house. In the 19th century, mourners kept a vigil over a body from death until burial and the funeral service was conducted in the house. Another Victorian mourning practice was to shroud all mirrors with black fabric upon someone's death in the house. This ritual kept the departed's spirit from getting trapped in the mirror.

Mrs. Roger's spirit avoided entrapment in a mirror and her ghost remains free roaming the confines of her former home.

2 Hauntedhamptons.com

THOMAS HALSEY HOMESTEAD

249 S Main Street

In 1640, Thomas Halsey Sr. became one of Southampton's original founders when his family built the first farmhouse in Southampton. The village is named after the port city of Southampton in Hampshire, England and is the oldest English settlement in the state of New York. The Halsey Homestead exists as the oldest house still standing in Southampton.

The original settlers sailed from Lynn, Massachusetts, after leaving their native England. Arriving at today's Conscience Point, they obtained a deed for land from British authorities and later came to terms with the Shinnecock tribe.

In 1683, Thomas Halsey Jr. built the current structure using wood frame timbers from his father's house to build his own. The weathered 17th century farmhouse boasts wide-planked floors and hand-hewn beams.

Today the home exhibits life as lived 350 years ago in Southampton. The museum holds many Halsey family's furnishings. Outside, an orchard and a replica colonial herb garden bourgeons with culinary and medicinal plants, necessary for the household.

The historic Halsey homestead is also filled with spirits. A haunting can be the result of a tragic, violent or unexpected death. In 1660, Lion Gardiner penned the "Chronicles of the Pequot Wars." His account cites *three Indians involved in a cruel and treacherous murder of an English woman in Southampton.*

It is said, but not proven, that Elizabeth Wheeler Halsey was brutally murdered and scalped by three Pequot Indians at the site. The Pequot were an aggressive New England tribe who waged war against the Long Island Indians.

Algonquin Chief Wyandanch captured the marauding Pequot trio and handed them over to Southampton authorities. The natives were extradited to Connecticut, found guilty and hanged.

"Near this spot in June 1640 landed the colonists from Lynn, Massachusetts who founded Southampton—the first English settlement in the state of New York."

According to author Kerriann Flanagan Brosky, cold spots are common in the house which may indicate a spirit presence. Electronic voice phenomena (EVP) captured at the property include a man saying "Out," and the voice of an older woman says, "I'm tired." Mrs. Halsey's spirit may be trapped in time due to her untimely and traumatic death.

OLD POST HOUSE

136 Main Street

The property at 136 Main Street is the former Post House, Southampton's second-oldest structure dating to 1684. Nello Balan once owned the property and operated the restaurant known as Nello Summertimes at the site.

Balan claimed his ancestor was the 15th century Romanian known as "Vlad the Impaler." Vlad inspired Bram Stoker's classic novel *Dracula*. Did the owner's family history conjure the ghostly activity at the site reported by the building's caretaker?

Alvaro Simon observed strange phenomena at the white-clapboard Colonial house. The young man says he witnessed two ghosts dancing "like whirling dervishes," in an interview he gave to *The New York Times* in 2008.

One night Simon perceived a tall apparition in a corner, and a dark disembodied head in an upstairs window. The perceptive man also sensed an incorporeal being walking next to him. The caretaker claimed he regularly discerned the sounds of a wild party downstairs in the main dining room during the wee hours of the morning.

The Post family ran a boarding house at the property in 1824. Later operated by the White family after Sarah Elizabeth Post married Captain Hubert White. Captain "Hubie" spent most of his life on the high seas. When he retired, the old salt parked himself for hours on the front porch. When he spotted a pretty woman walk by he'd fire his BB rifle at her—his alternative method of pinching her bottom, according to the *Times*.

Alvaro Simon experienced a paralyzing, paranormal

force holding him down in bed that made his blood run cold. Silently reciting *The Lord's Prayer* became the only solution to his dilemma. Finally the invisible entity loosened his grip freeing Simon's body.

Efren Oyerbide, the restaurant's captain also attested to a strange event. He awoke to a loud racket as if a slew of people were talking. He couldn't figure out from where the noise emanated. On the wall he observed the shadows of what looked like an entire *parade* of people passing by.

BABY GHOST

GIN LANE

Historian Richard Barons offered a sad and spooky tale that occurred in a home on Southampton's Gin Lane.

A couple bought the 19th century dwelling, which featured a beautifully carved staircase, as a summer place. Eventually, the pair started to visit their home on weekends in the off season.

Relaxing in the living room one evening, they heard a strange noise, it sounded like something bouncing down steps. They looked but found nothing. For two years they owned the house but only stayed there in the summer when the house teemed with people. This time it was different, the house was quiet with only the two of them.

A few nights later, the bouncing noise on the stairs awakened the husband and left him baffled again.

Days went by and while attending a local gathering a fellow guest inquired, *"What house do you live in?"* Like many Southampton houses it's known by the name of the family who built it, so the man replies with the name. The guest counters with, *"Oh, that's such a tragic house."*

It turns out that a few years after the house opened, the

owners threw an extravagant party. Even though the couple's three-year-old son was attended by a nanny, he eluded her supervision. The baby crawled out of bed and fell to his death while chasing his errant ball that bounced down the beautiful staircase.

"It's as if there are varying degrees of life, some interwoven or entwined with your world, where there is a weird mixture of living in almost, you might say, two worlds in one. That's where you get your hauntings from...

That's where you get these souls who are close... so close to earth in their mentality, that at certain times, under certain conditions, they become visible to people on your side who are probably not mediumistic or anything like that at all, but who do see.

There are moments of time when it is feasible, under certain conditions, for certain souls, Earthbound souls, to become quite physical or visible. Indeed, if only people realised it, the power of the mind is such that anything is possible. Nothing is impossible to those who understand a little bit more."

—Alfred Frost, Communicator
The Leslie Flint Educational Trust

SCOTT COTTAGE

The Port of Missing Men is a storied property constructed at Cow Neck as a hunting retreat by Standard Oil heir Colonel Henry Huddleston Rogers Jr. The unusual moniker derives from the 17 shipwreck victims who perished at the port in the early 1800s.

Overlooking Scallop Pond, architect John Russell Pope designed the Colonial Revival house, inspired by the cottage built on the spot in 1661 for Captain John Scott.

In the late 1600s, the harbor functioned as the most active port on Long Island and the third busiest of all the colonies behind Boston and Philadelphia. The area was known as Feversham and eventually became North Sea. A brick kiln and the Scott Cottage are all that survive the era.

The Scott Cottage belonged to the notorious Captain John Scott (1634–1696), a 17th century royal adviser, cartographer, military leader, spy, land speculator, and scoundrel who wanted the Island to be the 14th colony with himself installed as governor.

The Port of Missing Men was built around Colonel Rogers' hobbies, hunting and partying. During Prohibition, a liquor drop existed on the bay at the end of North Sea Road. Later, the liquor drop turned into a house of ill repute.

Rogers's grandson, the late Peter Salm, inherited the estate from his mother, Millicent Rogers, a fabled style icon and the daughter of Colonel Rogers. Salm became noted for his stewardship of the wetlands surrounding Cow Neck. Today, Salm's widow, the Countess Wiltraud von Salm-Hoogstraeten, also known as Willi Salm, owns the property.

In an article in the *Southampton Press* by Annette Winkle, Salm said Colonel Rogers gave every bedroom a name including a diminutive chamber upstairs in the 1661 Scott Cottage that he labeled "The Room of the Haunt."

Ms. Salm contends the aptly titled room is truly haunted. *"All my guests have seen a ghost in there,"* she told the *Sag Harbor Express.* The tiny room is spirited by the apparition of a young girl. She appears wearing a long white dress. Ms. Salm said the Scotts birthed a child every year but not all of them survived. The ghostly girl is one who perished.

Ms. Salm went on to say that she always runs late for appointments but feels certain her deceased husband has a hand in helping her out. When she has to be somewhere on time, he slams his bathroom door, from beyond the grave, to wake her up.

BYRAM HOUSE

JERMAIN AVENUE

The unique Italianate structure overlooking Oakland Cemetery was home to astronomer and clockmaker Ephraim N. Byram. Born in Sag Harbor on November 25, 1809, Byram descended from a family of clockmakers. A voracious reader, he too became a clockmaker as well as an astronomer, bookbinder, cabinetmaker, inventor, mechanic, and philosopher. The self-taught man crafted compasses, telescopes and other nautical instruments, which he constructed with tools he designed himself. Sag Harbor whalers would have literally been lost without Byram.

At the age of twenty-five he completed a mechanical model of the solar system called an "orrery." Best known for clock making, particularly tower clocks, the inventor designed steeple clocks for the Sag Harbor Methodist Church, the Old Whalers' Church, Manhattan's City Hall, and the U.S. Military Academy at West Point, among others. A Byram grandfather clock stands in the John Jermain Library; other items are on display at the Whaling Museum.

His Italianate Revival style villa with a campanile stands in front of the site of the Sherry & Byram Clock Works, which produced large clocks for church steeples and street posts all along the East Coast. Built by his father in 1852, Ephraim and his wife, Cornelia Pierce, who was a Spiritualist, lived in the quaint cottage. Topped with an asymmetrical tower, the diminutive room provided the amateur astronomer with an observatory for viewing the heavens. Each evening and into the wee hours of the morning, Byram peered at the night sky through his telescope. The stargazer stood six foot six inches tall and was an unforgettable sight roaming the village streets wearing his two-foot-high stovepipe hat.

After Byram's death in 1881, his wife Cornelia, who practiced homeopathic medicine, held séances in the house to conjure her husband's spirit. In the mid-1800s, séances were popular during the rise of Spiritualism. Early Spiritualist séances were dramatic and theatrical, taking place in darkened parlors around circular tables. Cornelia's séances incited rumors that the house was haunted. Locals, including their children, purposely crossed the street to avoid passing by the unusual house.

Byram's house is not traditionally haunted but, theoretically, anyplace where the spirits of the dead were conjured in séances has been visited by spirits from the unseen world.

OLD WHALERS' CHURCH

44 UNION STREET

Completed in 1844, the Old Whalers' Church was erected as a monument to Sag Harbor's whaling prosperity. The Egyptian Revival style house of worship is the town's most distinguished landmark. The church exterior is the best example of the Egyptian Revival style in the United States today. The structure's ornamentation includes a blubber-spade motif along the roofline.

The place of worship is the third edifice on the site—the present church is a far cry from the original Old Barn Church of 1766. The wood-frame, unfinished building lacked walls and a ceiling. When it rained during a service, the minister needed to move from the pulpit to escape the raindrops.

Initially, the present church was topped with a 185-foot steeple visible to ships rounding Montauk Point. The spire served as a welcome signal and the building achieved the status of the tallest structure on Long Island when built. The steeple was lifted off intact by the Great New England Hurricane of 1938 and smashed into the Old Burying Ground.

In 1994, the Old Whalers' Church became a National Historic Landmark and placed on the National Register of Historic Places.

PRESBYTERIAN CHURCH
SAG HARBOR, LONG ISLAND, N.Y.

The dangers of the whaling industry brought riches and specters to the south shore.[3] It appears that some whaling era spirits anchored at the holy spot... The choir loft is the epicenter of the church's haunting activity. Church organists use mirrors to observe the liturgy in order to know when to start playing the music. One evening, as an organist practiced alone, she caught sight of two distorted faces on either side of her when she looked into the organ mirrors. She said it looked like the faces were melting; they slowly faded away.

Once, the building's caretaker became mysteriously trapped in a crawl space when the door slammed closed and locked. Fortunately, with MacGyver-like ingenuity, and his screwdriver and flashlight, the worker removed the door hinges and freed himself.

A faithful parish member put in a post-mortem appearance in the choir loft the night he died, the parishioner's specter easily detectible by his long beard.

When paranormal crews investigated the property, batteries in their ghost hunting gear drained of their power upon entering the organ loft yet worked perfectly after exiting the area.

Visitors sometimes hear people talking around the church when no other mortal souls are present.

Those who've experienced the paranormal at the site endure eerie feelings when the sound of footsteps echo in empty rooms. Some discern disembodied shadow people

---

3 Todd Atteberry. "The Haunted Hamptons and Ghosts from the Sea from Long Island's South Shore." gothichorrorstories.com.

moving among the pews. There are those who consider shadow people to be a form of guardian angel. It makes sense they took up residence in the holy space.

JOHN JERMAIN MEMORIAL LIBRARY

201 MAIN STREET

As I spoke with librarian Susann Farrell over the phone about the haunting activity at the John Jermain Memorial Library, our conversation became punctuated with the noise of a rotary phone dialing. We both enjoyed a chuckle over the unusual anomaly, wondering where such an old-fashioned sound would come from in this day/age of high technology. Perhaps our call tapped into a time warp... Nevertheless, Ms. Farrell was gracious enough to provide the following fascinating essay about her paranormal experiences at the haunted library:

"Our building was first opened on 10/10/1910. It was a gift to the community from Mrs. Russell Sage, who also donated Pierson High School, Mashashimuet Park and eventually her home across the street from the library (currently the Whaling Museum). The building is named in honor of Mrs. Sage's grandfather, Major John

Jermain. He had served in the Westchester Militia during the American Revolution and reportedly was involved with George Washington.

Mrs. Sage wanted something beautiful to look at from her porch, so she paid the owners of the land a 'whopping' $10,000 as well as the cost to relocate their house. Augustus N. Allen designed the library building in the Classical Revival style. A brick, copper and stained glass dome rises sixty feet above the ground, constructed by the R. Guastavino Company. The stone lintels of the windows are designed with the Greek key pattern. In the interior, fluted stone columns, and lintels ornamented with medallions form the octagonal third floor reading room. Other architectural details include wreaths, torches and egg and dart molding. The building has a very spiritual look and feel to it. It was the "Fung shui" of Mrs. Sage's day!

I've mentioned the history and structure because it has a lot to do with the "feeling" of the building. Everyone says it has a comfortable, welcoming, homey feeling. I think that the spirits we have here choose to stay because of that atmosphere. The second floor was originally the main circulation area, but is now used as the children's department.

When the first ghost hunting team, Long Island Society for Paranormal Research, investigated in October 2006, their psychic medium picked up on children playing in the area. An electronic voice phenomenon recording, made late at night, caught children's voices saying, 'Stop it' and giggling. (This recording was on their website, and may still be). At the second investigation a year later, my then 7-year-old daughter Catherine and I were present. By using a K2 meter, we were able to "communicate" with these children. My daughter asked questions, and the K2 meter would light up once for "yes," twice for "no."

The two (ghost) children were school age, about 7 or 8. They wanted me to read them a story, so I read from a book for a little while. They seemed to love being in the children's area, but avoided the third and first floors. The interaction continued for about 20 minutes, but then they stopped responding. When we asked if they were afraid, they responded "yes." The "old man" was looking for them on the landing between floors. This grumpy old man was another spirit reported by the medium in 2006.

He goes back and forth between the third floor and the first (really the basement). I have heard people say they have felt someone sit next to them while working on the third floor. On the first floor, my co-workers Aracely and Rita saw a wheeled chair suddenly roll away from a computer and across the floor.

In October 2008, the New York Ghost Hunting Team spent several hours investigating. My own personal experience with the library's ghost was in the back area of the first floor, near the boiler room. This is the "dark spooky corner" of the basement, just where you would expect a ghost to hang out. Again with the use of a K2 meter (which indicates electro-magnetic fields), several of us were able to communicate with a spirit. This time it was the grumpy old man. He indicated he did not like people bothering him in the library. But when I asked if he was lonely, the K2 lit up like a Christmas tree! I felt deeply sorry for him.

There are also rumors that the building may be haunted by John Steinbeck, who lived in Sag Harbor. These rumors are perpetuated by an accurate, yet spooky looking, bust of the famous author located on the third floor.

MURF'S BACKSTREET TAVERN

64 DIVISION STREET

From 1760 to 1850, Sag Harbor bustled as a thriving whaling port. As a seaport, Sag Harbor ranked in importance second to New York City. During the lusty whaling days, 35 bars existed on Main Street alone. A liberated woman before her time, Betsy Jose ran a tavern that enjoyed a world-wide reputation.[4]

Established in 1792, Murf's Backstreet Tavern is Sag Harbor's oldest continuously running tavern. The bar is located a short stroll from the waterfront on the road that used to be called Tinker Alley, and at the time, the watering hole was known as Tinker Alley Tavern. This local, legendary landmark is known for its lively evenings, and ring toss.

A lot of the wood used to construct the tavern was repurposed from old whaling ships. Early axe marks remain

---

4 Dennis Starin. "Sag Harbor Tries to Preserve the Past While Welcoming the Future." *The New York Times*, July 8, 1973.

visible on the wood beam ceilings. In the basement, the original 18th century stone foundation exists, constructed without mortar. The ghostly resident upstairs remains invisible, but makes its presence known in tangible and mysterious ways.

In 1976, retired NYC police officer Tom Murphy purchased the humble dwelling to house his tavern. The late owner served as proprietor for over 30 years and sensed the spirits at Murf's consisted of more than the liquid kind.

Murphy believed the spirit of former resident, Adelaide "Addie" King, kept watch over her home from the great beyond. Addie was only 33 years old when she died. Maybe her untimely death is what keeps her spirit earthbound.

Murphy claimed the blender once turned on even though the switch was still in the off position. He also said Addie flipped chairs and even turned on the jukebox while Murphy performed a television interview. One time a glass flew off the overhead rack and landed into Murf's outstretched hand. Murphy stood just as surprised as his jaw-dropped patrons.

AN APPARITION
& THE LIGHT

When the English arrived on Long Island's South Fork in the mid-17th century, they discovered deep water on the bayside, a suitable port to moor oceangoing vessels burgeoning with cargo.

Overtime, the large meadow facing the wharf took on the name Sagaponack Harbor. Eventually the name became shortened to Sag Harbor and by the mid-18th century, houses appeared on the horizon.

Sag Harbor quickly evolved into a great whaling community and became a trendsetting village. The town boasted the first seaport in the region and was home to the first U. S. Customs House on Long Island. Sag Harbor introduced the island's first newspaper and launched the enterprise of delivering fresh milk to people's front doors.

The bustling village teamed with people from around the globe. Harboring ships held crews of American Indians, Polynesians, runaway slaves from the South, Africans and Aboriginal people from Australia.

At the time Sag Harbor was like no other place in America.

In an 1843 history of New York, the author stated there were only two places of any significance in the state, Brooklyn on the Island's West End and Sag Harbor on the East End.

Given such a background it's no wonder that spirits still make their home in the historic town. Richard Barons, Chief Curator at the Southampton Historical Museum, is a collector of true ghost stories and he shares his spooky tales with the public at various Long Island venues.

Sag Harbor's ghost connoisseur shared an eerie tale about a historic home on Main Street.

During the night, visitors heard a noise in the hallway that woke them up. The bedroom turned freezing cold and filled with the aroma of exotic incense. The occupants' gaze fell upon the closed bedroom door... it's oddly transparent— they can see the light right through it...

An old woman, dressed in a flannel nightgown and cap, stood in the doorway. The gaunt ghoul stood perfectly still, staring straight ahead into the room. Moments later, the room warmed up, the scent dissipated, and the ghost dissolved.

Barons said this haunting has occurred since the 1930s. To this day, unnerved guests arrive at the breakfast table eager to share their chilling experiences over a cup of strong coffee.

Another spooky story involves a house with eyebrow windows in Sag Harbor's Historic District. Back in the 1950s, the owner left the house to run errands. When she got into her car she noticed a faint light in the attic. For years, no one ventured into the garret and, now that she was thinking about it, the attic was not wired for electricity.

Concerned about a sparking wire in the 1860s house, the woman went back into her home to check upstairs. Her inspection fortunately found nothing amiss. The woman locked up the house and gave a glance at the house. A light no longer glowed in the decorative window.

A week later, a neighbor mentioned that he noticed a light on in the woman's attic night after night. Totally baffled, the woman went upstairs again and carefully inspected the eaves. Eventually, she discovered a 19th century oil lamp sitting on a crate facing the window over the front door. She took the lantern downstairs to the living room.

One night she awoke to a loud noise; it sounded like a branch hitting the window. Unable to sleep she went downstairs, peered into the parlor, and saw the oil lamp was lit!

Totally perplexed, the woman rationalized that the light she observed was merely the reflection off the lamp's pewter surface. Nevertheless, to allay her nagging misgivings, she consigned the lamp to a closet and forgot about it.

Several years later the woman rented out her house and flew overseas.

During her European stay, she received correspondence from the tenant. He expressed concern about a light coming from under the closet door. The woman knew exactly what the light source was, but the closet door is locked rendering the tenant unable to help.

Upon her arrival home, she immediately sold the lamp to a local antique dealer.

Paranormal specialists contend that antiques or used items such as furniture, jewelry, statues, or *lanterns*, can carry energy imprints or spirit attachments from former owners or environments.

MAIN STR. and SOLDIER'S MONUMENT, Sag Harbor, L. I.

In 1895, The New York Times reported that young men observed a six-foot-tall ghost, with a musket and long hat, while the young women of Sag Harbor remained indoors.

EAST HAMPTON

GREY GARDENS

3 W End Road

Private Residence

In 1913, Robert C. Hill and his gardener wife Anna Gilman Hill, purchased the 1897 dwelling designed by Joseph Greenleaf Thorpe. Anna worked with landscape architect Ruth Bramley Dean to design a walled garden. Dean imported decorative concrete walls from Spain to protect the yard from the harsh Atlantic winds.

In 1924, Louise Shelton included the walled garden in her book, *Beautiful Gardens in America* where Anna told Shelton, *"It was truly a gray garden. The soft gray of the dunes, cement walls, and sea mists gave us our color scheme as well as our name."*

That same year, Phelan Beale and his wife Edith Ewing Bouvier Beale (paternal aunt of Jacqueline Kennedy Onassis) bought the house. The Beales separated in 1931, with Edith retaining the house. In 1946, the Beale's divorced. In July 1952, Beale's daughter Edith (known as "Little Edie") returned, after five years in Manhattan, to live permanently at Grey Gardens.[5]

5   Eva Marie Beale. *Edith Bouvier Beale of Grey Gardens: A Life in Pictures*, 2008.

Once a vibrant debutante, Little Edie turned reclusive and lived with her mother in one room of the sprawling house. Without the means to maintain the premises, the property fell into ruin and became overrun with cats and raccoons, infested with fleas and piled high with garbage. Albert and David Maysles recorded the sad state of affairs in their documentary *Grey Gardens* (1975).

Lois Wright was a good friend of the Beales and stayed with them for 13 months. An artist, palm reader, and tarot card reader, Ms. Wright lived life as a free spirit. She used the kitchen as her art studio to capture daily life at the cottage.

Ms. Wright acknowledged she slept in a room frequented by a spectral sea captain.

For years, Little Edie spoke of nocturnal appearances of a sea captain to her bedroom. She claimed they were lovers and every night he climbed a ladder to her upstairs room. She insisted the visits occurred and repeated the story throughout her life. Her nighttime paramour, however, existed only in spirit.

The otherworldly seafarer is not the only apparition ambling about the place, other spirits are afoot in the celebrated house.

Sally Quinn and Ben Bradlee bought the dilapidated

estate from Little Edie in 1979. They restored the house and lived there together until 2014. In an interview on CNBC, Quinn stated she observed an apparition in her bedroom at night, one of two ghosts in residence. The ghost of Little Edie, who died in 2002, was a regular. Quinn also woke up in her bedroom and witnessed the apparition of Anna Gilman Hill the horticulturist who designed the gardens at the summer cottage.

Quinn said every night around 10:00, the hall lights would flicker once. Announcing the ghostly presence? Even though the ethereal occupants are harmless, when guests heard disembodied noises, they refused to stay in Little Edie's bedroom. Quinn felt certain the unearthly company was the sea captain because of the noise his ghost made stomping around the room in boots.

> *"For who can wonder that man should feel a vague belief in tales of disembodied spirits wandering through those places which they once dearly affected, when he himself, scarcely less separated from his old world than they, is forever lingering upon past emotions and bygone times, and hovering, the ghost of his former self, about the places and people that warmed his heart of old?"*
> —CHARLES DICKENS

SOUTH END CEMETERY

34 James Lane

The 1st Lord of the Manor of Gardiner's Island, Captain Lion Gardiner founded the first English settlement in New York State. His descendants still hold title to the island.

Lion Gardiner (1599–1663) is the oldest burial in South End Cemetery. His gravestone, however, is not the original. In 1886, architect James Renwick Jr. designed Gardiner's sarcophagus. Gardiner's effigy is carved in stone depicting him as a medieval knight. (Renwick also designed St. Patrick's Cathedral in Manhattan). Many generations of the Gardiner family rest within this graveyard.

A spooky, oft told tale involves one of Gardiner's daughters. Elizabeth fell sick with a mysterious illness and the girl accused Elizabeth "Goody" Garlick of using witchcraft against her. ("Goody" was a term of address shared by lower status females). Fortunately, the woman was acquitted in 1658 and lived a long life. some believe Goody Garlick is buried somewhere within the graveyard.

There is a ghost haunting the graveyard, however. The

spirit is the daughter of the miller who worked at the nearby
Gardiner Windmill.

OSBORN JACKSON HOUSE

101 Main Street

The Osborn-Jackson House is a period house museum named for its first and last owners. The oldest portion of the structure dates to 1723. Six generations of the Osborn family lived here until the late 1960s.

This colonial house is situated in its original location on Main Street, and is owned and maintained by the Village of East Hampton. In 1977, Lionel Jackson donated the property to the village for use as a museum. The structure serves as the headquarters for the East Hampton Historical Society.

The interior is furnished with over two dozen pieces of furniture made by the same local craftsmen family who also built two of the village's windmills. Chairs, cradles, chests, and a tall case clock, are among the local furnishings decorating the place.

One year, during the holiday season, the alarm system began to blare at six p.m. This anomaly occurred every day for a month. The police, security personnel, and the museum director responded each and every time. The motion sensor in the dining room activated for no known reason.

For years rumors swirled that Frances Huntting haunted the Osborn-Jackson house. "Aunt Fanny" never married. She lived with her sister Mrs. Mary Osborn in the house in the mid-19th century. Aunt Fanny was a well-loved figure in the community.

In the 1880s, Fanny's health began to fail, and she became confined to the house. Despite her inability to walk, Aunt Fanny remained upbeat and positive and was often visited by her many friends and well-wishers. Most times, Fanny received her guests in the elegant dining room. She situated herself in a comfortable chair and watched life go by on Main Street.

Many Osborn-Jackson House workers witnessed a woman in Victorian-era dress looking out the dining room window.

Sometimes staffers caught a whiff of lemon verbena, a favorite of Fanny's, when walking through the dining area.

All agreed Fannie's spirit was truly alive and well in her mortal abode so lovingly cared for by the historical society. Does Fanny's spirit stay behind to show her approval that the home continues to welcome visitors? Perhaps her spirit returned and tripped the alarm to show her earthly friends that she is alive and well, albeit in another dimension.

30 EGYPT LANE

Private Residence

Founded in 1648, farmers and fishermen journeyed across Long Island Sound to East Hampton to secure a way to live off the land and sea. Early East Hampton was governed by righteous, religious leaders similar to Massachusetts' control by the Puritans. Witches and witchcraft trials occurred hundreds of years ago here, but the level of hysteria never came close to the terror provoked in Salem, Massachusetts.

Until the beginning of the 20th century, farming and fishing prevailed as East Hampton's dominant livelihood, but the town began to earn a reputation as a refuge from urban life and soon attracted wealthy families, artists, and writers.

Actress Renée Zellweger once owned the renovated farmhouse at 30 Egypt Lane. Originally, Benjamin and Hannah Worthington purchased the East Hampton property "down Egypt," in 1884.

Back in the late 1600s when Egypt Lane received its name, the location was known for its deep sand rendering the road almost impassable. The lane became an important thoroughfare for both whalers and fishermen on the way to the sea.

The couple gave birth to 16 children and Lillian

Worthington was the last to survive. Lillian worked as a bookkeeper at the East Hampton National Bank. She passed away in the house on Egypt Lane when she was 94 years of age in 1962.

The four-bedroom, three-bath dwelling is haunted by Lilian Worthington's spirit according to a former owner. Furniture designer John Mascheroni lived in the gray-shingled home for eight years and said the female spirit loved to play tricks.

When John started renovations on the historic structure, Lillian showed her displeasure in a number of ways to the changes in her earthly home. One night as John lay in bed, he sensed her presence and felt like "there was a large block of ice next to me."[6]

Another time, as he discussed canning vegetables in the kitchen with friends, a book fell off a nearby shelf—a book about canning and preserving.

Worthington's spirit eventually settled down when she realized the new owner wasn't making drastic changes to her former abode.

6   Dan Kadison. "Hamptons Diary." *The New York Post*, July 28, 2003.

Renée Zellweger is not the only celebrity to once reside in a spirited home on Long Island's South Fork. In 2014, The New York Post *published a report that singer/songwriter Billy Joel encountered the apparition of a 19th-century woman brushing her hair in his former East Hampton home. Joel revealed his ghost sighting during an interview with shock jock Howard Stern. Joel sold the property to Jerry Seinfeld in 2000. Seinfeld has yet to say if he's spotted the spirit—not that there's anything wrong with that.* ☺

MILL HOUSE INN

31 N Main Street

In 1851, the ship *Catherine*, wrecked off the Amagansett coast. The ship carried 300 Irish immigrants who were all rescued by the steamer *Achilles*.

Colonel William D. Parsons approached one of the male survivors on the beach and offered him work on his farm. Patrick Lynch planned to go west in search of gold, but he changed his mind and accepted Parsons' job offer. Lynch prospered, and in 1860, purchased the property at today's 31 N Main Street.

No Catholic churches existed in East Hampton in the late 19th century, so the Lynch family held services in their home every other week. "Farmers and former first ladies attended the services—Julia Gardiner Tyler was a regular."[7]

After the coming of the railroad, Patrick and family opened their home to boarders. In 1973, family descendants sold the home and a succession of new owners continued to operate the Mill House as an inn.

Some say Patrick Lynch still inhabits his former home, albeit in spirit form. Shortly after purchasing the inn (on a

7 Millhouseinn.com

Friday the 13th in October with a full harvest moon), all the inn's electronics went haywire. the printer became erratic, the telephone system turned bonkers, (the main lines rang in the guest rooms), and voicemail went kerflooey.[8]

Communication specialists insisted a power surge did not cause the anomalies. The owners feel their resident ghost must have discovered the wonders of modern technology.

8 Millhouseinn.com

OLD MONTAUK HIGHWAY

Traveling east on Old Montauk Highway, slightly past Amagansett, there's a stretch of road haunted by a little girl ghost. Many have spotted her, not only on the highway, but also walking down the beach. Sometimes she's seen walking on the highway with her mother.

Todd Atteberry posted an eerie tale about an encounter with the waif's wraith on his website, gothichorrorstories.com:

"I could remember what she was wearing clear as day. She was in a dark red dress with white trim and a white bib style front to the dress. Her hair was brown and was up in a ponytail.

She turned to look at me, but before our eyes could lock I slammed both feet on my brakes. My car slid at least 15 feet until I heard and felt two distinct bumps in my steering wheel. I became frozen by the idea of running a child over since I have six nieces myself."

When the driver nervously got out of his car to check, no one was there.

MONTAUK MANOR

236 Edgemere Street

Supernatural stories swirl about the sprawling Montauk Manor perched high on Signal Hill.

More than any other individual, Carl Fisher made his mark on Montauk. After successfully developing Miami Beach out of a mangrove swamp, the industrialist who also created the Indianapolis Speedway, turned his sights to the East End of Long Island where he envisioned the most fabulous summer resort ever imagined in the western world.

In 1926, the multi-millionaire and four partners purchased 9000 acres on the Montauk peninsula. The centerpiece of his exclusive summer resort was an English Tudor style luxury hotel. The 178-room lodge became a magnet for the rich and famous.

Work on "Miami Beach of the North" began with forming Montauk Harbor. Fisher dredged a channel between what was then Great Pond and Block Island Sound to create a marina and launch his yacht club.

The fashionable resort sported a beach club, polo fields, golf course, glass enclosed tennis courts, a half-mile boardwalk along the ocean, a ranch, and health spa. Restaurants served internationally acclaimed cuisine. Croquet players sported on the meticulously manicured lawns. Afternoon tea was sipped on the veranda overlooking the dreamscape. In short, Montauk Manor was the ultimate in opulence.

Life was good for Fisher and his lavish undertaking until 1929 when the Great Depression forced his development company into bankruptcy.

The resort revived in 1933 and operated for 30 years as a hotel but again financial difficulties shut its doors.

For over 20 years the brooding behemoth sat empty atop its elevated outlook, a victim of vandalism, a sad and spooky landmark. In 1981, investors rescued the property and by 1985 a $20 million restoration project was complete. Montauk Manor regaled in its original splendor and beauty.

That's when the weirdness began.

As stated in the article, "What Haunts Montauk Manor" by Amanda Star Frazer of *The East Hampton Star*, a female staffer witnessed a male figure bathed in bright light walk by the door. She described him as tall with long white hair. There was something unusual about this stranger who stared directly at the captivated worker as he passed by her office. Thinking someone unauthorized was entering the employees' area, she ran to follow the man, but he was nowhere to be found.

Ghostly sightings occurred on all floors mostly during the off-season at dawn, dusk, and during the night.

A female guest claimed that one night her bed lifted five feet off the floor while she was in it affirmed another employee. The woman moved to a different room right after the incident.

A golfer awoke in his room to find a Native American in full headdress standing at the foot of his bed. His two roommates, disturbed from their sleep by his screams, also witnessed the apparition who suddenly departed before their eyes.

Another guest, wrapped in a towel, ran to the lobby and excitedly described a specter peering down at him from a heating vent as he showered. Investigators found nothing amiss. A local tradesman who worked in the manor one winter took photos of his work. When they were developed, one shot revealed a white haze, there was no such fog when he took the picture. Ghosts may be identified through mist or energy in photos that is not visible with the naked eye.

The rambling resort endures sitting adjacent to Fort Hill, site of an ancient native stronghold. Below lies Massacre Valley where the Montaukett tribe waged war with the Narragansetts in 1654. Montauketts buried their fallen brothers on the Great Hill and their descendants allege contractors desecrated the most significant Native American burial ground on the northeast coast.

Not only natives perished here; in the 1890s, Theodore Roosevelt escorted a regiment of his "Rough Riders" soldiers to the site. Quarantined with yellow fever in a temporary hospital that stood where the Manor's parking lot exists, many perished and were temporarily buried on top of the tribal remains.

Perhaps the Native's spirits resent the intrusion upon their land and continue to protest the loss of their territory.

MONTAUK LIGHTHOUSE

The Montauk Point Lighthouse is the oldest lighthouse in New York State. Authorized by President George Washington in 1792, the lighthouse was completed on November 5, 1796. The historic beacon still serves as a navigational aid and became a designated National Historic Landmark in 2012.

The famous lighthouse is haunted by the ghost of a young woman named Abigail. Her spectral voice echoes in the tower, the vocal sound audible over the crashing waves. Some of her other post-mortem actions include pictures swaying on the walls and the noise of furniture being moved around.

In 1811, a destructive storm ravaged New York and Long Island, laying waste to ships and ports. Nathaniel Prime described the carnage in in his *History of Long Island* (1845):

"The remarkable snow-storm of December 23rd, 1811, was the most destructive of both life and property of any that is known to have occurred on the northern shore. The preceding day was remarkably warm and fair. The change

took place suddenly in the night, the mercury falling almost to zero. A snowstorm commenced, accompanied with a tremendous wind, which lasted without intermission for 24 hours. Between 50 and 60 vessels foundered in the Sound, or were driven on the northern shore of the island in that terrible night. In some cases, the entire crews perished, while in others, those who survived, were objects of greater commiseration than the dead, being horribly frozen. The writer can speak with entire confidence on this subject, as he was an eyewitness to some of the ravages of that awful tempest. About 20 perished within 10 miles of his residence, 4 of whom, from one vessel, he assisted in burying, on Christmas day and in administering to the necessities of 3 wretched survivors of the same crew. The bodies taken up from the shore were completely covered with ice of an inch in thickness, through which the features of the face appeared in all the ghastliness of death. That storm will never be forgotten by the last survivor of that generation...."

On December 24, 1811, a teenaged Abigail Olsen washed ashore from a shipwreck. Sadly, she perished from her injuries inside the lighthouse. There are several versions of the story, but lighthouse keeper Joe Gaviola's version seems to align with the haunting activity.

Gaviola relates that Abigail and the captain of the ship that wrecked were newlyweds. Abigail managed to survive the wreckage near the lighthouse, and made her way to the tower. She frantically searched for her husband and was unable to locate him. Legend says that's why her spirit stays behind—she waits and watches for his return.

Gaviola also hears her disembodied voice and other inexplicable noises in the keeper's house and some objects go missing.

Henry Osmers, Montauk Lighthouse Historian, told the *Southampton Press* that one day as he climbed the spiral staircase before opening for visitors, he heard the distinct sound of a motor—it sounded like a vacuum. When he reached the top, no one was there. When working in the archive room, twice Osmers felt a distinctive tug on his jacket. He wanted the unnerving experience to end, and he told the spirit to stop. The spirit complied and Osmers went on with his work undisturbed.

As Osmers gave a tour to students near an exhibit about lighthouse keeper Jacob Hand, a picture on the wall suddenly moved back and forth by itself. Once as Greg Donohue, of the Montauk Historical Society, explained the legend of Abigail to guests, the watch tower door flew open.

Margaret Winski is a former, longtime lighthouse keeper who lived on-site. She said the attic and cellar turned eerie after sundown. Her dog refused to enter the basement at night, perhaps sensing things that we humans cannot. When a museum director felt a cold breeze brush past him in the attic, he raced downstairs.

The atmosphere at the lighthouse is charged with the possibility that one is not truly alone at the historic beacon.

WICKHAM FARMHOUSE

MAIN ROAD

For eleven generations, Wickham's Fruit Farm has stood on the Main Road in Cutchogue offering hungry visitors a delicious taste of North Fork life. The Wickham family's long history in Cutchogue stretches back to the 1600s. The farm features the oldest cider mill on the North Fork, dating to 1902, as well as the earliest farm stand, which opened in the 1940s.[9] Sadly, their family history also includes a gruesome murder that occurred almost two centuries ago.

On the night of June 2, 1854, Nicholas Bain, an enraged Irish farmhand, murdered James and Francis Wickham in their bedroom.

Known to have a drinking problem, and an eye for girls, Wickham terminated Bain's employment when the worker became infuriated after a young woman rejected him. In fact,

9 Lisa Finn. "Wickham's Fruit Farm, a Beloved Family Business for Generations, Looks to Future, Holds Deep Ties to Past." Patch.com, July 1, 2016.

not only was Bain terminated, when he refused to leave the farm, Wickham evicted the ne'er do well.

Shouting revenge all the way to the train station, Bain changed his mind and ditched the train ride. He turned on his heels and decisively trudged ten miles back to the farm. Arriving under cover of darkness, Bain grabbed a poleax and stealthily entered the home where he proceeded to commit the murders.

When news of the awful carnage spread throughout the town, residents flew into action. Bain's murder incensed the wrong crowd. The Wickham family was well-respected in the community. Armed with all sorts of weapons, a manhunt immediately ensued. A fatigued Bain was no match for the angry mob. He was apprehended, stood trial and was found guilty of the murders. Bain hanged in Riverhead for the crime.

"Bain's body was taken down, placed in a wooden coffin and brought to the south side of the Peconic River to a place named Egypt. He was buried in an unmarked grave."[10]

In 1988, 134 years after the killings, descendants Anne and John Wickham awoke to a dark, spectral figure standing over their bed brandishing an ax. The terrified couple sealed the room which remains closed to this day. Some say you can still hear Nicholas Bain's disembodied, angry footfalls emanating from the second-floor hall.

---

10 Kerriann Flanagan Brosky, *Ghosts of Long Island; Stories of the Paranormal.* Maple Hill Press, 2006.

MATTITUCK

OLD MILL INN

5775 West Mill Road

The historic Old Mill Inn is a former gristmill completed around 1820 by Samuel Cox. His tidal mill on the Mattituck Inlet took five years to complete. The dam, mill, and gates operated day and night. The incoming tide forced the gates open at mid-stream. During ebb tide, the gates closed, and an auxiliary gate opened through a tunnel, turning the mill once again.

The unique mill operation found its way into the Library of Congress and was recognized as a rare engineering feat. The millstone still exists at the site and the driveshaft still stands as a pillar in the structure.

In 1902, the mill was purchased by Yetter & Moore, a Riverhead-based soda and beer bottling firm. The company converted the mill into a convivial eating and drinking establishment. Otto Magdefrau managed the restaurant and encouraged patrons to carve their names on the beams— their engravings still visible in the building. Magdefrau also entertained the clientele with his animals. Stories still circulate about the beer-drinking monkey who lived in the water tower bathroom.

A 1906 storm destroyed the tidal dam, so a swivel bridge was installed to allow boats passage up the creek. Bar patrons often helped move the bridge for yacht traffic. In 1955 the bridge was condemned and destroyed.

During Prohibition, Mattituck Inlet became a popular route for rumrunners; tales of bootlegging are legendary. The Old Mill's kitchen still boasts a drop door that enabled boats to obtain illegal alcohol during low tide.

The tavern grew into a romantic hideaway offering Clark Gable and Carole Lombard seclusion when they, and others seeking privacy, escaped to the shelter of the old inn.

The restaurant and bar opened in 1939, and 20 years later, Mr. and Mrs. Richard Holmes ran the place. Mrs. Holmes passed away sometime during the 1970s. She may have died but did she cross over…?

According to Barbara Pepe, one of the inn's former owners, Mrs. Holmes was a woman of her era—with a taste for dry martinis! After her death Mrs. Holmes developed a fondness for gentlemen sitting at the bar. Particularly, she liked to grab their legs or tickle their ears.

Several Old Mill Inn patrons experienced Mrs. Holmes' cool presence and post-mortem interest. Though deceased for nearly four decades, Mrs. Holmes kept her hand in the business in other astonishing ways. She haunted the place by flinging the heavy ice scoop across the room. Serving trays moved as if by invisible hands as did the pantry door that opened and closed itself.

Her playful spirit caused pans to tumble from a shelf onto Judy Daly, a previous owner. About the same time, Daly became mysteriously locked in the walk-in refrigerator. Judy's husband Jerry said Mrs. Holmes used to turn on the stereo in the bar after he shut everything down and went to bed upstairs.

In 2006, shortly after the restaurant changed hands again, one of the new owners, Joanne Chando, personally encountered Mrs. Holmes:

"Mentally exhausted one of the Opening Nights, after working in the corner area where I later learned

Mrs. Holmes also kept her eyes and ears on the dining room—I was washing my hands in the single-use women's bathroom, felt someone behind me, turned and saw Mrs. Holmes. There was a very positive, calm atmosphere in the room, and I immediately felt that our decision to purchase the business was a good move!"

Barbara Pepe also caught an otherworldly glimpse. One evening after the dining room closed around 11:00 P.M., Barbara walked through the darkened space and peered to her right. Outside, a presence in white hovered over Mattituck Inlet. *"It wasn't light refracted from somewhere or anything that could be explained in any other way,"* she said. *"It was gone in about three seconds, but I understood it was Mrs. Holmes."*

Within the next two weeks, the chef at the time also witnessed the mystical Holmes. Looking out the kitchen window he observed a woman in white floating down the inlet. Jerry Daly used to keep a lobster tank in the restaurant. His young granddaughter took a photo of the lobsters and caught an ethereal Mrs. Holmes in the background. This type of evidence is the gold standard for today's ghost hunters!

Wade Karlin is a commercial fisherman and social studies schoolteacher. Years ago, after a long, hot day fishing out on the high seas, he and his nephew, Carl Nickerson, headed over to their favorite haunt for a couple of cold beers.

On this lazy, summer evening Wade sat turned to his right and casually chatted with a bar patron. He felt something flicking his left ear, so he brushed it away as if swatting a fly.

Again, he felt something playing with his ear. *"Cut it out,"* he admonished his nephew, but Carl was lost in thought and nowhere near his uncle's ear.

A visitor sitting at the bar who was poring over the inn's history book exclaimed, *"This place is haunted?"* At that precise moment, a shiver jolted Wade's body into an eerie awareness. He had heard the inn possessed a friendly spirit... now he shuddered in awe of her otherworldly touch.

As of this writing, the 200-year-old mill building is closed and sits empty. Or does it...?

> *"Next to the mill sits a lagoon,*
> *that releases spirits each full moon.*
> *The lagoon is but a shallow basin*
> *but becomes paranormal on a certain occasion."*
> —ALAN SPENCER

JAMESPORT MANOR INN

370 MANOR LANE

The Jamesport Manor Inn is a beautifully restored mansard-roof Second Empire style structure on Long Island's North Fork. The upscale restaurant maintains a spooky past—locals long avowed the place was haunted.

Matthew Kar bought the property in 2004. He meticulously restored the inn, focusing on details from the slate roof right down to the parquet floors. On an October morning right before the grand opening in 2005, the building burned to the ground. Investigators never determined the cause; they speculated a pile of rags spontaneously combusted.

Undeterred, Matt doggedly rebuilt. Today's Jamesport Manor Inn, or the "Manor Reborn" as the owners like to say, remains an architectural landmark. Its haunted reputation also remains intact.

The inn possesses a long and storied past including many owners and one incarnation as a brothel. The Dimon family acquired the property on Manor Lane in the 1750s. Jonathan Dimon (1727–1787) probably built the original house at that time. His son served in the Minutemen Militia during the Revolutionary War, and his descendants fought in the War of 1812.

One member of the family, John Dimon, was among the first to construct clipper ships, including the famous *Sea Witch*. He also built early steamships and raced them up the Hudson River against his friend and rival Cornelius Vanderbilt.

One of John's sons, John Franklin Dimon, became a successful South American merchant and eventually returned to America. He and his Peruvian wife, Rosalie, rebuilt his father's manor into the mansion recreated today.

The Dimons raised three children in the manse. Tragically, their 10-year-old daughter, Margaret, fell from a tree in the front yard and died. Hers is one of the spirits still attached to the property. Staff members spot her playful specter outside.

Neighbors sometimes drop by the restaurant to inform the owner they've observed a sad looking woman standing at the window when the restaurant is closed. After her daughter's death, Rosalie became a recluse and died in the house after enduring forty years of sorrow.

> *"There are an infinite number of universes existing side by side and through which our consciousnesses constantly pass. In these universes, all possibilities exist. You are alive in some, long dead in others, and never existed in still others. Many of our "ghosts" could indeed be visions of people going about their business in a parallel universe or another time—or both."*
>
> —PAUL F. ENO

SOUTH JAMESPORT

JEDEDIAH HAWKINS INN

400 S JAMESPORT AVENUE

Jedediah Hawkins Inn is a historic venue nestled amongst 22 acres of fragrant farmland, gorgeous gardens, and lush vineyards. The Italianate Victorian mansion is completely restored to its original Civil War era splendor.

Constructed in 1863 by Captain Jedediah Hawkins, a Captain in the Union Army, the house was rumored to be haunted when it stood vacant during the close of the 20th century. New owners purchased and renovated the property in 2004.

Some say doors open and close on their own and several employees experienced uncomfortable "creepy" feelings in the basement. Staffers believe Jedediah's presence, or other deceased Hawkins family members, still linger here.

The unobtrusive manifestations of former residents in any historic structure are part and parcel of a building's history and, this writer feels, adds to its ambiance. The bottom line here is a feeling of peace pervades the place.

According to the Jedediah Hawkins Inn's website, "Legends abound about the house; some claim that Jedediah Hawkins was an abolitionist and the house was a station on the Underground Railroad; others claim that Jedediah was a gunrunner. Although there is no historical evidence for these speculations, there are unexplained secret passages and trapdoors throughout the house, which pique our imagination and lend some support to stories."

AFTERWORD

The Hamptons' history as a dwelling place for the wealthy dates from the late 19th century when the community changed from a farming community with good potato ground to a popular destination. In 1893, *The New York Times* wrote:

> *"The beautiful villages clustering around old Southampton, including Quohue, Good Ground, the rest of the Hamptons, and the incomparable Shinnecock Hills combine to make as close an approach to Eden as can be found in a long journey. Exclusive—in the best sense of the word—society is here represented during the summer by its choicest spirits. Well-bred men and women find a congenial atmosphere, refined attractions in plenty, and innumerable charms about these quaint old villages."*

The towns that comprise the Hamptons are drenched in history… and ghost stories. Does the proximity to water assist the spirits to thrive here? Is it the beauty and/or convivial times keeping the spirits anchored here? We will never truly know *how* spirited the storied villages are because a lot of people are reluctant to talk about their ghosts. Understandably so. Real estate prices in the Hamptons achieve astronomical amounts. Some feel if knowledge of the energies from the past existing in their expensive home becomes public, that disclosure may affect them economically.

Indeed. Stambovsky v. Ackley, commonly known as the "Ghostbusters Ruling," is a landmark legal case where the New York State Supreme Court ruled in 1991 that if a house is known to be haunted that information must be divulged in any real estate transaction as a pre-existing condition.

When *The New York Times* interviewed a former director of the Southampton Historical Museum, he said, "*... anyone here with a haunted house tells their friends very coyly. You don't brag about a ghost here. It might screw up a real estate deal.*"

Some feel a resident ghost is a good thing while others don't like to talk about their ghosts for fear of ridicule. Whatever the reason, I have done my best to ferret out the phantoms of the South Fork using public sources and private interviews. I've also designated private residences as such and reinforce that ***trespassing is strictly forbidden.***

ACKNOWLEDGEMENTS

Authoring a book is a solitary endeavor that is never accomplished alone. I want to recognize all who helped me create *Haunted Hamptons*.

To Todd Atteberry—thanks for saying "yes." I value your artistry, research and time and feel fortunate your evocative photos illustrate some of the stories.

To K. Jackson Barnes for your dedication and transcriptions.

To Joanne Chando, Barbara Pepe and all the Old Mill Inn owners, thanks so much for your assistance and participation.

To Richard Barons, Chief Curator, and Marianne Della Croce, Director of Visitor Experience, East Hampton Historical Society.

To Susann Farrell at the John Jermain Library, thank you for your enthusiastic and careful chronicling of the library's ghosts.

To Wade Karlin for the gripping rendition of your ghostly encounter.

To Bobbi Torres for your morning research! Thank you for discovering and sharing such meaningful and relevant information.

To graphic designer Deb Tremper. Collaborating with you all these years… it's like you're family!

BIBLIOGRAPHY

Atteberry, Todd. "The Haunted Hamptons and Ghosts from the Sea from Long Island's South Shore." gothichorrorstories.com.

_____. "A True Ghost Story for Christmas: Abigail of Montauk Point Lighthouse." gothichorrorstories.com.

Bellows, Charles. "Return the Windmill." *Dan's Papers*, September 3, 2004.

Blanchard, Wayne. *Deadliest American Disasters and Large-Loss-of-Life Events.* www.usdeadlyevents.com

Bleyer, Bill. "Historian touts North Sea's forgotten port past." *Newsday*, June 12. 2015.

Brosky, Kerriann Flanagan. *Ghosts of Long Island.* Maple Hill Press, 2006.

Cassidy, Grace and Euler, Laura. "Haunted places in the Hamptons." hamptons.curbed.com, October 25, 2008.

Cohen, Lon S. "Things To Do In The Hamptons When You're Dead." hamptons.com, October 23, 2007.

DiNapoli, Jessica. "Paranormal investigator leads tour of haunted Hampton Bays store." *Southampton Press*, October 27, 2008.

Euler, Laura. "Did the Ghost of Anne Brontë Haunt a Quogue Staircase?" hamptons.curbed.com, December 30, 2014.

Fedor, Kristen. "Billy Joel Shares Hamptons Ghost Story with Howard Stern." *Dan's Papers*, May 6, 2014.

Fischler, Marcelle S. "Footsteps, Voices, Creepy Stuff. Uh-Oh." *The New York Times*, October 21, 2007.

_____. "Memories of a Former Resident of Grey Gardens." *The New York Times*, May 25, 2008.

Flammer, Joseph and Hill, Diane. "Haunted Inns of the North Fork." *Dan's Papers*, October 29, 2011.

Frazer, Amanda Star. "What Haunts Montauk Manor?" *The East Hampton Star*, October 25, 2001.

Gilbert, Colette. "An East Hampton Ghost of Christmas Past." *The East Hampton Star*, December 3, 2020.

Gould, Jennifer. "Ghost World—Grey Gardens: Quinn & Bradlee's Hamptons Haunt." *New York Post*, August 17, 2006.

Hinkle, Annette. "Chilling Nighttime Tales." *The Sag Harbor Express*, October 24, 2002.

_____. "Terrifying True Tales and Other Bumps in the Night." *The Sag Harbor Express*, October 3, 2003.

_____. "Got Ghosts? The John Jermain Memorial Library just might." *The Sag Harbor Express*, October 31, 2008.

Kadison, Dan, "Hamptons Diary." *The New York Post*, July 28, 2003.

Koppel, Lily. "In a Hamptons Inn Centuries Old, Perhaps More Guests Than Meet the Eye." *The New York Times*, October 26, 2008.

Macken, Lynda Lee. *Haunted Long Island*. Black Cat Press, 2005.

_____. *Haunted Long Island II*. Black Cat Press, 2009.

McGaffney, Ambrose. "Millicent Rogers and the Port of Missing Men." avenuemagazine.com, July 27, 2020.

Menu, Gavin. "Ghostly Tails From Favorite Village Haunts." *Sag Harbor Express*, October 24, 2017.

Peterson, Oliver. "East End Haunts are scarce but there." *The East Hampton Press,* October 29, 2009.

_____. "New York Ghost Hunting Team visits Sag Harbor library." *The Southampton Press,* October 27, 2008.

_____. "Hamptons Ghost Hunting Diary—Session 2: Thomas Halsey Homestead." *Dan's Papers*, October 23, 2013.

_____. "Top 5 Haunted Places in the Hamptons." *Dan's Papers*, October 26. 2016.

Scanlon, Mayra. "Exploring the South End Burying Ground." *East Hampton Star,* February 20, 2020.

Smith, Kyle. "12 Shocking Facts about Billy Joel." *The New York Post*, April 29, 2014.

Starin, Dennis. "Sag Harbor Tries to Preserve the Past While Welcoming the Future." *The New York Times*, July 8, 1973.

Staff Writer. "East End haunts are scarce but still there." *Southampton Press*, October 8, 2009.

_____. "What Lies Within 'The Room Of The Haunt' At The Port Of Missing Men?" *Southampton Press*, October 15, 2019.

Tanaaz. "The Real Paranormal." Undated. Foreverconscious.com.

Vespe, Elizabeth. "Some Say Abigail Haunts The Montauk Light." *Southampton Press*, October 29, 2018.

Wick, Steve. "Sag Harbor's Heyday." www.newsday.com.

Annie, Wilkinson. "Tales of the Ghosts at Grey Gardens." *Long Island Press*, October 25, 2021.

Zezima, Jerry. "In Spirited Company." *Newsday*, October 25, 1998.

WEBSITES

Behind the Hedges: behindthehedges.com/haunted-hamptons

Curbed Hamptons: hamptons.curbed.com/haunted-places-hamptons

Dan's Papers: danspapers.com

East Hampton: easthamptonlibrary.org

Grey Gardens Online: greygardensonline.com

Hampton Bays Historical Society: hamptonbayshistoricalsociety.org

Historic Halls of Mirfield: mirfieldmemories.co.uk

Jamesport Manor Inn: jamesportmanorinn.com

John Jermain Memorial Library: johnjermain.org

Kerriann Flanagan Brosky's Blog: kerriannflanaganbrosky.blogspot.com.

Leslie Flint Educational Trust: leslieflint.com

Mill House Inn: millhouseinn.com

The Old Mill Inn: theoldmillinn.net

Old Whalers' Church: oldwhalerschurch.org

Southampton History: southamptonhistory.com/ghosts-evidence

Villa Paul Restaurant: villapaulrestaurant.com

Wikipedia: wikipedia.com

PHOTO CREDITS

Also by Lynda Lee Macken

Adirondack Ghosts

Adirondack Ghosts II

Adirondack Ghosts III

Catskill Ghosts

Empire Ghosts, Historic Haunts in New York State

Ghost Hunting the Mohawk Valley

Ghosts of the Jersey Shore

Ghosts of the Jersey Shore II

Haunted Cape May

Haunted History of Staten Island

Haunted Houses of New Jersey

Haunted Houses of the Hudson Valley

Haunted Lake George

Haunted Lake Placid

Haunted Long Beach Island

Haunted Long Island

Haunted Long Island II

Haunted Monmouth County

Haunted New Hope

Haunted Salem

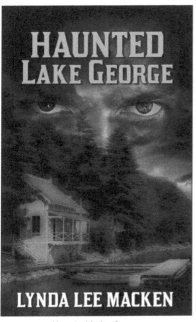

Haunted Lake George

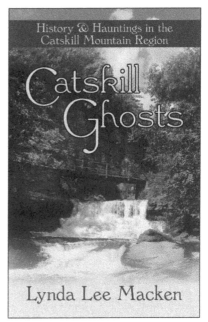

Catskill Ghosts

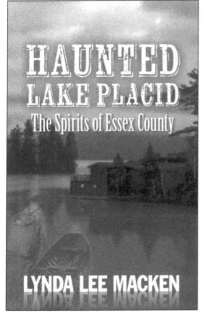

Haunted Lake Placid

Adirondack Ghosts

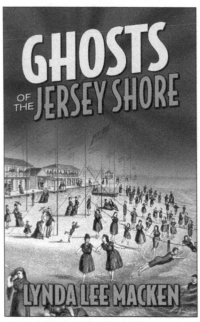

Ghosts of the Jersey Shore

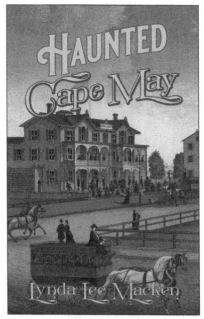

Haunted Cape May

Haunted Long Beach Island

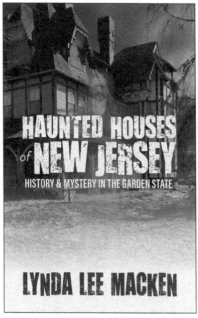

Haunted Houses of New Jersey

Made in USA - Kendallville, IN
73014_9781736006948
05.02.2022 1434